For Kathy,

from Marj (Marge Elder)

Each time we touch in spirit

we grow stronger.

INTO THE SILENCE

HEALING THE WOUNDS OF ABUSE

Marj

White Oak Publications
Victor, New York

White Oak Publications
Post Office Box 567
Victor, NY 14564-0567

First printing
10 9 8 7 6 5 4 3 2 1

Publisher's Cataloging in Publication
(*Prepared by Quality Books Inc.*)

Marj.
Into the silence : healing the wounds of abuse / by Marj.
p.cm
Chiefly poems
1. Abused women—United States—Psychological aspects—Biography. 2. Sexually abused children—United States—Family relationships—Psychological aspects—Biography. 3. Psychotherapy 4. Autobiography—Women authors. I. Title. II. Title: Healing the wounds of abuse.

HQ72.U53 364.153
QB191-1484

ISBN 0-9630388-1-8 : $9.95
LCC 91- 68074

Printed and bound in the United States of America

This book is dedicated with much love and respect

to my little girl

to my therapist
who helped me find her

and to my family:

my daughter—whose courage helped lead the way

my son—who reminded me of my first amendment rights

my mother and sisters—who listened

and you, my husband,
thank you for seeing me through the night.

PERSONAL ACKNOWLEDGMENTS

The support, encouragement and instructive feedback I have received from friends and strangers has been incredible. I thank them and wish I had the space to list all their names here.

I would like to make special note of the following people for the time and knowledge they have contributed. Without them, I would never have finished the book:

Bonnie G., "therapist from Jersey," who facilitated several of the marathons with Terry. Her presence underlies all my work.

My friend Judy, who brought her knowledge of poetry and art to bear on my writing. Her editorial comments and evaluation of the organic structure and design of the book has been invaluable. I treasure her friendship, respect her honesty, and appreciate her instinctive awareness of the raw impulses from which my words spring.

Bob Herzog, writer and teacher, for his willingness to read and comment on my writing. His expertise and sensitivity helped me look at my work from an artistic perspective. After reading his comments, I began to be able to say I wrote "poetry" without stuttering over the word.

Dona Bagley, graphic designer, for the beautiful work she has done for me.

Amy and John Hughes, my poetry's conduit to the world. Their support prompted me to show my writing to other people.

My fellow travelers in groups and marathons throughout the past three years. You know who you are. Thank you for listening to my poetry.

Pamela C. Rodgers, M.S.Ed., Therapist, and her client, whom I've never met and to whom I feel so close; Carole Blocher, survivor of sexual abuse, woman of great strength; Carolyn Cerami, CSW, ACSW, who gave me a totally new perspective on my writing; Bonnie and Pat, two women who bring such graceful strength and sensitivity to this world; Wendy Beller-Madway, Psychotherapist, Board of Directors—New York State Coalition Against Sexual Abuse; for reading and commenting on the final manuscript.

Marnie Hodil, Kim Keefe, Sylvia Matteson and Chauncy Young, who read various drafts and offered insight into the work.

Harvey Carapella and Dorothy Hoskins, instructors at Rochester Institute of Technology, for introducing me to the language of design and printing.

Jeanne Gehret of Verbal Images, for her willingness to answer my questions about publishing.

Dan Mooney, attorney-at-law, for counseling me with such sensitivity around the issue of liability.

Geoff Tesch, photographer-guitarist-cabinetmaker, for providing a window into his creative world and helping me believe I belong.

Deirdre Rosenberg, of Oser Press, for giving such care to the printing of the book cover and offering me encouragement in moments of panic.

Maharishi Mahesh Yogi, whose meditation technique has enabled me to work through this issue at such a deep level with power and simplicity.

To all of you, thank you.

Contents

Personal Acknowledgments - 7
Dear Reader - 11
It all started with my daughter - 15
IntoThe Silence - 21
"I guess I thought you loved me." - 23
Marjie lived - 25
My heart was bruised - 27
Long ago - 28
Daddy - 30
My little girl's world - 34
We have to go back again - 36
"There is no such thing as a 6-year-old whore." - 37
I didn't just crawl from an egg - 39
Rage - 40
I invited my father to my room - 42
I am angry - 43
I'll whittle it slowly - 44
To my husband - 45
"I'm scared," - 46
It should be easy - 48
It is so silent - 49
I seek peace - 51
My battle is not of muscles - 53
I know how my mantra works - 54
Moonlight slips like silk - 55

Group - 57
- You can't fool me! - 59
- When I spoke of tinsel and lights - 60
- To M— the "willful child" - 62
- Terry counsels - 65
- The marathon - 66

"Are you scared?" Marj asked. - 69
- I need to see you needy - 71
- I did it! - 73
- So what's the big deal? - 74
- Run away with me - 76
- It was your birthday - 79
- The fire I built was white heat - 83

I hear your voice - 85
- I am a woman of the earth - 87
- Daddy - 89
- How could such a small truth - 92

Dear Reader - 95

Letters - 97
- Dear Bill - 99
- Dear Marj - 101
- Dear Bill - 103
- Dear Marj - 105
- Dear Bill - 106
- Dear Marj - 108
- Dear Bill - 109
- Dear Marj - 110
- Dear Reader - 111

Dear Reader,

My sisters and I, my mother, my father, lived for awhile in a hell born of events that occurred long before my time. For years we struggled to bring a semblance of sanity to our lives, each in a different way, each building a small space of safety. We tried to move away from the past, although I felt its tentacles pulling at me constantly, sometimes subtly, sometimes with a force I found overpowering.

Then I went into therapy and started to write. The images came tumbling back, evoking shadows none of us wanted to see.

I didn't share my writing with my mother and sisters until I began to think of publication. Actually, since early childhood I hadn't shared much of anything with them. I was an escape artist, tantalizing them with little glimpses into my heart, running away when they began to respond. But suddenly, with my poetry, our lives and my work had become inextricably linked.

They listened to my poems. It wasn't easy for any of us. I was petrified, envisioning all sorts of horrible consequences from reading my work to them: heart attacks, suicides and—most frightening of all—closeness. They were deeply disturbed by what I was telling them. And they were dismayed at the thought of publication.

With my therapist's help, we created a space in which we could all meet. What a gift they gave me with their willingness to take this risk. I don't mean to suggest that they have accepted my claims of sexual abuse as The Truth. But they have listened and thought and questioned and heard my pain. Throughout it all, I have tried to be honest, to not run and hide. We are becoming a family that talks, cries and laughs together, ripping away heavy shrouds that have weighed us down for years.

We might never be whole. The wounds cut to the quick. But I take hope from the fact that my own daughter's courage to heal has given birth to a fuller life for the two of us. We are honest with each other. We blunder through a new way of relating, hurting at times, laughing at times, testing the width and breadth of our relationship. For me it is a joyous celebration.

Why does it seem that love is built on a foundation of grief? In my childhood fantasies, I thought that love somehow erased pain. Now I see it differently. The sorrow I feel when I think of the tragedy of my family is deep. It swells in my consciousness from time to time, its richness flavoring my life, bringing a passion that I treasure. Recognizing that sorrow, I can love.

I didn't know I had to find the pain in order to feel the joy, to cry in order to smile, to rage in order to be tranquil.

I didn't know I had to go into the silence to sing.

Is it unfortunate that my song is so public?

Perhaps. Perhaps not. I can't answer that question. Ironically, the knife-like honesty of my writing that I thought would kill my mother has actually brought new life to our relationship.

And what of my father?

He made a decision years ago to put the past behind him. His home is several thousand miles away across the United States and across an inner space that he doesn't want to bridge.

After three years of therapy, I wrote to him telling of my memories. I included some of my poems in the letter because I thought they best expressed my feelings. He said the events did not happen. He does not want to talk about it. I am saddened—but not surprised. He always found discussing feelings too upsetting. Should things be different now? He has, however, given me permission to include his letters in this book.

Why have I chosen to publish under "Marj"?

I have talked about my memories in the place where it counts: the family. I also talk quite openly to other people. The shame is his, not mine; I don't whisper when I speak of it. But I have decided not to wave a red flag over my father's and mother's heads.

This decision was not made lightly. I sought legal opinion, therapeutic opinion and opinion from friends. In the end, I have done what feels right to me. It is a compromise. Sometimes it scratches at me, and I have to look again. But I haven't changed my mind.

And now to you. The journey you and I are on is long. I hope you'll find something in this book that makes the passage less lonely. Don't read it all at once. Approach it as you would a twenty-course meal. Sit with a poem. Savor it. Dive into its heart if you wish. Let it melt on your tongue like sweet whipped cream. Or, if it burns like a jalapeño pepper, spit it out.

Whatever you do, I hope it helps.

Marj

✧ ✧ ✧

It all started with my daughter, Laura. The healing, that is. She told me of a therapist she was seeing who was into all sorts of bizarre things like tablework and twelve-hour-long sessions called marathons. People cried and hugged and "gave each other support" or batted (batted???!) a punching bag during this work.

"I'd really like to do a marathon with you," she said.

"No way!" I said.

The image of all those feelings flying around a room scared me. What was the point of wallowing in one's misery? I had been to a therapist several years earlier and had reached a plateau of comfort. My anxiety seemed under control, although my sudden flares of anger and attempts to maintain a safe emotional distance from everyone were disconcerting. Why stir it all up again?

No, she'd never get me to a marathon. But one 50-minute session with Laura and her therapist? Why not? Nothing beyond my control would happen there.

I hated Terry* immediately, with his deep voice that pulsed like a mantra in my ears, with his warm smile and soft eyes. I didn't trust him as far as I could throw a ball of cotton.

We talked. And they described the tablework to me. The client, said Terry, lies on a padded table and closes her eyes while he asks questions and at times gently touches....

"You let him touch you?" I said to Laura, an hysterical note in my voice.

And then I looked at him.

"I'll kill you if you touch her legs!" I said.

Well! I thought. Where did that come from? Kill him?

Eventually, we did a marathon together. Laura and I, along with ten other people, closeted ourselves in a room with Terry for twelve hours and "worked" on our issues. Work it was! People role-played family themes, using Terry's therapy paraphernalia as props. They swung foam bats, tried to let go of (umbilical cord) ropes, and did floor- or tablework in search of their wounded inner child and emotional freedom of action in their lives. Throughout it all, they turned to each other or to Terry for support and comfort with a simplicity and emotional honesty I'd never seen before.

The marathon worked wonders for Laura. She no longer felt attached to me from the top of her head to the bottom of her soul, not knowing where she began and I

*My therapist's name and the names of others in this book have been changed for reasons of confidentiality.

ended. It wasn't difficult to understand the change. In the first half hour she saw me deteriorate into a frenzy of fear and anger, kicking and hitting objects within my reach and screaming at Terry that I'd kill him if he got near me. By lunchtime, I had developed an intimate relationship with the mass of black beetles devouring my gut. Ten hours later, I slipped like slime out the door.

Not exactly an auspicious beginning!

The next day I made a private appointment with Terry, the first of many weekly sessions.

I started to remember my lost years, my childhood that had fallen into a crevasse so long ago. Horrible memories flashed like still images in my mind's eye. At the center was my father—touching where he shouldn't touch, showing what he shouldn't show.

The people housed in my body*—mischievous three-year-old, abused six-year-old, defiant ten-year-old, uncertain teenager—flung themselves through therapy sessions, trying to condense 49 years of life into one 50-minute session. Like a flash flood surging down a dry, cracked riverbed in the Arizona desert, they would burst on the scene without warning, cutting new courses through the hard surfaces of my perception, exposing raw feelings and pain with a power that exhilarated and frightened me. And always there was Terry, whom I alternately attempted to seduce or threatened to beat to a pulp as I offered up various shades of rapture and torture depending on the time of day, the humidity, or what I had eaten for lunch.

As I clawed my way through the fire and fog, when

*Terry's therapeutic approach involves finding one's inner children and teaching you, the adult, to give them the love and support they never had. When I speak of "my little girl" and "my teenager," I am referring to these "children."

moments of clarity gave me respite from the wild bombshells of emotions, we met, Terry and I, and talked about it all—he with his cup of coffee and chewing gum, I with my herb tea—the shadows and echoes of each battle still palpable in the room. These lucid moments of conversation gave me hope.

✧ ✧ ✧

I began writing letters to Terry for release. It was my way of climbing out of the emotional abyss, of relieving the pressure in my head, a pressure that at times made me press my palms against my temples as if trying to contain an explosion.

I would start by pacing the house, hands thrust in my pockets, walking faster and faster around the dining-room table, mumbling or shouting a phrase over and over and over. Then I would sit down at the computer and begin to write. I knew the experience would be a white-water raft ride through Level 5 rapids, with me clinging to the side screaming in terror, fearful I would die of a massive stroke before I even had the chance to drown in the water pounding my face.

Yet something about the rush that came over me whenever I wrote from the heart kept me writing.

Shame and embarrassment never hit until after the mailman drove off down the street with my letter tucked safely in his bag. When I envisioned Terry reading what I had written, I wanted to die. In my mind, I would begin to whip myself to a quivering mass of bloody flesh or cut myself with knives for thinking my words and feelings were worthy of expression.

And so it went.

The time came when I wanted to share my work with others. I chose the people well, friends who recognized my struggle as familiar, friends who were searching for answers to the sadness in their own lives. They said my words touched them and helped them find some clarity and light.

And they talked of publication.

Publication?

"Never," I said.

I wasn't ready to deal with that moment when the book went to print and was suddenly out of my hands. Publication would be the ultimate coming out. Would it be followed by an unbearable shame? Would I shrink from the eyes of friends and strangers, embarrassed by my momentary belief that my writing fit somewhere in the world, that I fit somewhere in the world?

My little girl was frightened; my teenager aghast.

"I'll be so ashamed. I'll go into hiding. My writing's no good. It's not poetry. It's junk!"

"But these poems are my feelings; these poems are my art. Don't they deserve a forum?"

"What if I hurt myself? What if I die?"

Thus began an endless struggle in my mind as the part of me that believed in my writing fought what seemed at times to be an uphill battle against tormenting feelings of panic and shame:

"Oh God, the publicity!

"How could I do that to my mother? She'll kill herself."

"Keep it a secret. Publish under a pseudonym."

"Hypocrite!"

"Spineless weakling!"

"But my father. He'll die of a heart attack."

"He'll sue me."

For more than two years I felt drawn and quartered as my urges to protect people fought against a steady move in the direction of publication. "What if's" and "How can you's" dominated my internal conversations. It seemed as though I'd stepped across a line into a place where nothing was tangible. How could I maintain the illusion of control in a world where figures were not yet drawn, speeches not yet written?

So much has happened since those first thoughts of publication. I've talked honestly with my mother and sisters. I've confronted my father with my memories. I've learned to trust my instincts. Fear tugs at me from time to time but doesn't paralyze me. I no longer wander in circles, stepping toward everything and reaching nothing.

Why?

I told my truth,
and no one died.

✧ ✧ ✧

Into The Silence

"I guess I thought you loved me."

Marjie

✧

Marjie livedwith her mother, her two sisters and her father in a house in a beautiful woods of dogwood, oak and beech trees.

Every day Marjie's father went to work. In the evening, she would hear the five-o-clock whistle blow and know that her father would be home for supper. She was always happy when he came home.

They would all sit at the supper table. Her father usually had one beer with his supper. Marjie hated the smell of beer. Her mother would make conversation.

Marjie's mother got very sick. She couldn't take care of anyone anymore. Marjie's father had lots of women friends. Once he put his arm around one of his friends. Marjie saw him and thought, "He loves her." He didn't love Marjie's mother.

Sometimes at night Marjie's father came up to her bedroom to rub her legs. She liked him to do that because the muscles were so tense. One night he rubbed more than her legs. She didn't like that as much.

Marjie really lived in a portable box. She had lived in the box for a long time, longer than she could remember. She always put the box over herself before she left her room in the morning. It was made of invisible stuff that helped her stand tall.

Sometimes people stared, trying to figure out how she could stand so tall. They couldn't see the box, and she didn't tell them about it because then it would collapse.

Marjie felt the house was too crowded. Sometimes clouds of poisons would float through the rooms. She was glad she stayed in her box, because it helped her be alive. Everyone else seemed to sink down to the floor like collapsed balloons.

They would all sit at the supper table. Her father usually had one beer with his supper. Her mother would make conversation. They all hated each other and pretended they were sane.

One day Marjie's father ran away from home. He went to live with one of his women friends. Sometimes he would come and visit, and Marjie hid in the woods.

Marjie's mother got a job. It was very quiet in the house. One of her sisters disappeared somewhere. Marjie could see her sister's ghost walking around, sitting at the table and lying on the couch being tired.

There was thunder in Marjie's head.

Every day Marjie walked through the house trying not to trip on the limp bodies of her sisters. Sometimes her mother grabbed at her and tried to suck her under. She ran away as fast as she could. Her mother and sisters thought she was mean.

But Marjie was strong. She didn't need help. She lived in her portable box.

✧

✧

My heart was bruised,
so I cushioned it in cotton,
put it in a box,
and hid it where no one could find it.
I fought to keep it safe.
When the pain was too great,
I let it feel the sun and wind
and let it laugh with friends.
I bathed it in music,
and it sang with the pulse of the universe.

This morning I found my heart,
soft and warm and as pure as before the pain.
But it is tender and
touching must be gentle.

✧

✧

Long ago,
or so it seems to me,
a little girl sang of kitten heartbeats and
dandelion chains,
her three years resting lightly on her shoulders.
Indian paintbrush and autumn leaves splashed
bright colors on the canvas of her dreams,
floating
with the music of her mind.

In the fairyland that was her playground,
she held her silver sword aloft,
taming creatures
whose icy breath
dared to turn the sun into a frozen golden orb.

When she was six,
her father brought her darkness
with a touch that should be foreign to any child.
She gathered up the fragments of her dreams
and sucked them deeply in
where they were safe,
where she could hold them to her heart
and feel,
from time to time,
their pulsing life and warmth
that would not die.

But she no longer sang,
because her songs were dark,
because the pain from singing was too great,
because no one heard
even if they tried to listen.

✧

✧

Daddy
Your paper airplanes were special.
You didn't simply fold the paper
'til it looked like it would fly.
You cut the shape you wanted,
sculpting its form
with the same intensity and playfulness
you brought to everything.
We flew test flights to check the aerodynamics,
adding a paper clip for weight,
until the plane would fly across the room,
gliding to rest on the floor
or crashing into the opposite wall.

And the glory of the music you drew from our Steinway!
Chopin and Beethoven pulsed
through your powerful hands,
swelling my heart and soul until
they burst the boundaries of what I knew,
filling me with a passion for life
and teaching me to fly.
Your fingers would caress the keys,
the sweetness of Mendelssohn singing
through the open window,
accompanying my dance with the butterflies,
my courtship with the wind.

You were different from the other fathers,
and I loved you.

When you came into my room,
I thought you were another man.
I couldn't see your face.
"Daddy?" I said,
and then relaxed
because I saw that it was you,
although I didn't understand
why you had come.

My hand felt safe between your legs,
buried in your softness and warmth.
But when I looked I saw hair and darkness,
and you kept swelling up until
you were so big and hard
I didn't know what to do.
I was afraid
and wanted to burrow under the covers
until you went away.

When you touched me,
your fingers playing me as they did the piano keys,
it felt good.
But I was afraid
and tried to disappear.

I guess I thought you loved me.
I thought I'd won the battle,
that I had left the others far behind
as I always had when skiing
or climbing
or running through the woods.
Yet my heart was slowly suffocating
in the filth you brought to my bed.

I felt blackness in my body,
and somewhere along the way
I lost myself.

I don't think you ever knew what loving was.
A puppet to your own horrors,
you survived at my expense,
blindly seeking pleasure for yourself,
never thinking what you might be doing to me.
I was a new avenue to explore,
dessert
after eating other foods you'd found at hand.
How convenient
that you only had to walk into my room,
instead of wandering the streets in search of sex.

I thought I had to push you down,
to bloody you with knives.
But I was wrong.
I'm the one who's holding on.

When I push, I push against myself,
ending in a stalemate
because I don't know who I want to vanquish.

I'm frightened.
But I'll be damned if I'll wrap myself in soiled sheets
and wait for you to die.
You can have the filth and shame.
I'll keep the passion,
and dance my ballet with the wind.

✧

✧

My little girl's world is a series of exquisite moments,
of love, of hurt, of excitement, of pain,
of whirling leaves,
diving into each to the exclusion of all the others.
She runs from one moment to the next
with exhilaration,
getting such a thrill out of being
that it's awfully hard to sit still.

Even in the photograph,
foot on the pedal of her tricycle,
ready to shove off
after having to sit for a 250th of a second,
flirting with the camera, a devilish gleam in her eye
—come on, I've got to move so I can ride around the circle ten times seeing how far I can go how long before I have to stop then throw myself on the grass roll down the hill as I catch my breath......I can hang by my knees from the trapeze, turn cartwheels, walk on my hands, do twenty-two somersaults without stopping—

Only the horror of betrayal makes her panic,
wandering blindly in the twilight zone
of our father's making,
hands outstretched
to feel the walls of the cave,

shivering
at a shifting of air currents,
a rabbit frozen in its tracks
by the shadow of a circling hawk,
calling out for a saviour
silently
so no one would hear
and discover her in her shame.

She's somersaulted through it all
and landed on her feet.
I'm going to cut away the straitjacket
and let her be.
I want the rawness of her emotions alive
so I can go to the fountain at will.
But I'd also like to drink from china teacups,
chuckling to myself as she fidgets
and looks for a floating tea leaf that means
a stranger's going to visit.

We need to negotiate an agreement,
she and I,
with the understanding that I'm the one in charge,
that I won't let her get lost
in a maze of moments.

It's a matter of respect.

✧

✧

"We have to go back again," I said.
"I know," she said,
and I wondered at the wisdom of such a little girl.
"Will it hurt?" she asked,
though I could tell from her voice
she already knew it would.
"Remember how it hurt so much you wanted to hide?"
I said.
We sat for awhile without talking,
thinking about the last time and the first time,
and we cried.
"I'm afraid to be alone with the shadows," she said,
moving closer to me.
"I know," I said, "but this time I'll be with you.
Do you trust me?"
She turned and looked at me,
measuring my strength and honesty
against other betrayals in the past.
"I trust you."
"We won't go until you're ready," I said.
"I'm ready now," she said, standing up, chin high.
"You're very brave," I said and stood up with her.
We held tightly to each other's hands,
knowing that it was time to go.

✧

"There is no such thing as a 6-year-old whore."

Terry

✧

I didn't just crawl from an egg at the age of twelve.
Shadows of my youth,
horrible shadows
that make me gag and hide in corners,
are forming in the void.

The remembering has begun.

Now I know why I am not surprised by cruelty
from those I love.
Now I know why I build barricades
to ward off physical contact.
Now I know why I am frightened of sex.
Now I know why I am swollen with rage.

Damn, it's good to know these things!

✧

✧

Rage

The child found it
in the morning before the dawn,
the time of monsters
when the warrior's armor is in the closet,
and the only thing that protects is Luck.
It loomed beneath the fog,
rising steadily,
silently pushing its way into view,
offering up a promise of violence and pain.

Like an undetonated bomb of the London blitz
or mines in the killing fields of Cambodia and Vietnam,
the mammoth depth charge lay waiting,
its timing device ticking steadily to a rhythm
set during a war years ago.
Perhaps an ant in search of sugar
would wander across the detonator,
the pressure of its tiny legs
sufficient to explode the charge.

The child curled into a ball
and waited for the dawn
when
maybe
she would be safe.

The warrior was long in coming,
dragging herself slowly from the immobilizing blanket
that had settled over her limbs
an invisible web
weakening her resolve and drugging her to indifference.
But she did come   and told the child to step back.

She eyed the object with respect,
searching her mind for
Procedures to Defuse a Dangerous Explosive Device,
knowing that the survival rate
of bomb squads in England
left much to be desired.

Should she make a little hole in the surface?
Let the contents seep out in whispers?
Or should she give the damn thing a kick
and ride with the explosion,
hoping that people wouldn't be scraping up her remains
for years to come?

The warrior turned to the child
and saw that she was gone,
wandering through the fields in search of raindrops,
jewels for the tiny fairies that live in the flowers.

✧

✧

I invited my father to my room.
I said, "Come upstairs and rub my legs."
because the muscles were like twisted knots
and needed
the kneading of strong fingers.
We played games in my bedroom
my father and I
while my mother lay in her bed
sick
near death
unable to stand and fight back.

I am a six-year-old whore
seducer of my father
violator of my soul.
With the hypocrite's tongue
I preach a higher moral code
look down on those who fall below.

I—seducer of my father
violator of my soul.

✧

✧

I am angry.

Angry that my father did such terrible things to me.
Angry that my mother was blind.
Angry that I lived in terror for so long.
Angry that I had no one to cry with.
Angry that my family couldn't laugh together.
Angry that I had to fight my own battles.
Angry that I was taught to not express feelings.
Angry that my spirit has been drowning in fear
and uncertainty for so many years.
Angry that Laura is suffering because of this shit.

I am goddamned ANGRY.

How DARE my father have done those things to me.
How DARE my father have done those things to me.
How DARE my father have done those things to me!

Never again.

✧

✧

I'll whittle it slowly
as I would a large stick
sitting on an upturned log
feet apart
my forearms resting on my knees.

I'll whittle it slowly
the weight of my knife
familiar to my hand
the blade still warm
from the whetstone.

I'll cut it away
layer by layer
until all that remains is a flaccid tube
hanging like a sodden piece of cold spaghetti
between his legs.

I'll clean my blade in the rich earth
and then walk away
leaving him standing alone
his filth dripping down his legs
forming a sticky puddle at his feet.

✧

✧

To my husband

When I was a woman,
I ran my fingers down your body
and discovered a mole hidden
by the curly hair at the base of your penis.
You cupped my breasts in your hands
brushing my nipples with your lips.
We smiled
shivering with the pleasure of it.

Now,
as a child,
I lie rigid on the mattress.
You caress me,
your hand closing in on my breast.
You touch my nipple
piercing my soul.

My father's hand is under the sheets
and the bed is too crowded for love.

✧

✧

To my husband

"I'm scared,"
you said,
and I wanted to hold you in my arms as I would a child,
murmuring words of comfort to take away the tears.

But I didn't.
Our path together is strewn with worn masks
of mothers and fathers and needy children.
They lie on rocks and grasses like molted snakeskins,
flapping in the wind,
gradually disintegrating into nothing.
We carry replacements on our backs,
an infinite supply of faces,
some for you and some for me.
We're not fussy about who puts what on whom.

You and I are struggling,
throwing around sex and poetry,
treading on each other's spirits in such subtle ways
with sarcasm and smiles,
when all the while our blood is seething
with a slow boiling anger.

I've been a chameleon for years,
changing colors

with the times and people that I've known.
But at this juncture,
as we begin to look within,
I find I've tired
of the shifting landscapes of my being that,
like sand dunes sculpted by the winds,
swallow up the flowers and little creatures at their base.

I'm sick of masks,
of mothering you in my flights
from intimacy and understanding,
of blaming you for something that my father did.
I'm leaving that behind,
stripping the burden from my back
and tossing it into the chasm
that almost swallowed up my past.

I'm not your mother,
nor are you my father.
Why can't we love each other simply
as a woman and a man?

We've chosen different ways of seeking,
and there are times when I'm afraid it won't work out,
that years from now
all our pathways to each other
will be twisted ruts that fade off as mirages
in the desert of our lives.

✧

✧

It should be easy—
Telling my mother the truth, I mean.
It's what mothers and daughters do, isn't it?
Talk together about boys and bras and
what happens when you become a woman?

But it isn't easy.
I'm too frightened to pick up the phone.

If I show her my heart
she'll devour me as she would a ripe plum
my juices dripping from her elbows
sucking me in until there is nothing left
except a faint imprint on space
which even I cannot see.

✧

✧

It is so silent,
this throbbing ocean of sorrow
that she has brought to me.
Before today
when I felt its current pull me in,
I struggled to escape because
I feared I'd drown in that living silence.

Yet she,
a child engulfed,
has lived as if it were a nurturing womb,
choosing the safety of solitude,
knowing that I offered a crushing brittle love,
born of shame,
destined to destroy.

She was a portal to the sufferers of the world,
and I passed through with arms outstretched,
looking neither left nor right,
not knowing that the cries I heard were hers.

✧

I seek peace
a peace so pervasive
I can listen to the hum of insects in the fields
for pleasure
not just for relief of pain.

Marj

✧

My battle is not of muscles
and screams
and cutting with knives.
It is a quiet battle of the spirit,
a turning   here and there,
a tugging   in the directions of either purity or filth.
With purity comes innocence.
With uncleanliness comes a suffocating cloud,
and I must use all my energy to keep from smothering.

The blackness in my body,
the seething mass of little beetles in my gut,
that feeds upon itself
and the rottenness of me,
thrives on the filth,
spreading within me
until,
if unchecked,
it will become me.

But my heart can eradicate the beetles,
enveloping
their grinding mandibles and sucking tongues
with a light that can grow
until,
if unchecked,
it will become me.

✧

✧

I know how my mantra works in meditation.

I know that spiritual realizations come not with force
but rather through letting go and trusting the process.

I know when beauty is true within me
and when I am holding on to a fleeting experience.

I know that holding on to either beauty or filth
brings strain into the system.

I know this with my awareness as well as my intellect.
I recognize when I am holding on
and can flip a switch to redirect the energy.

I know the power of the heart.
I know that it flows in the universe
and cannot be destroyed.
I need to give it space to flow within me.

✧

✧

Moonlight slips like silk
into the pores of the earth,
illuminating the aster-white hill,
a galaxy of curves and hollows.
Stars brush my legs,
quivering in my wake
as I wade through the Milky Way...
I am soothed.

✧

Group

"You talk to me even after I reveal myself to be such a monster."
Marj

"Well, we all think we are monsters, don't we?"
A—

✧

You can't fool me!
I know you're there,
'cause when I called for you to play
I saw the curtain move.

You're at the window,
chin an inch above the sill,
eyes squinting in the one thin beam of light
you've just let in your room.

Perhaps you're wishing you could run outside,
imprisoning your demons in the dark,
so that when we're making angels in the snow,
we won't be swept away
in a storm of cries and curses.

Don't be afraid.
I have a magic playground
with a warrior standing guard.
Come on over,
and we can close our eyes,
tip our faces to the sky,
and let snowflakes kiss our cheeks.

✧

✧

When I spoke of tinsel and lights
I thought
(as a child thinks her pleasures will please all)
I'd given you a treasure
you could hold when you were sad.
But
when I spoke of tinsel and lights,
you cried.

What do you mourn with your tears?
Did your little-girl dreams
of fairylands and magic,
of palaces that glisten with diamonds and gems,
die young?
Did they collapse from blows
of a wrecking ball
wielded by false prophets,
who preached deliverance from Hell
even as they made a hell for you?

Like Peter Pan trying to save Tinkerbell
I call out for you to believe
in fairies
who offer sweet drinks
and gentle lullabies,
who sprinkle sparkling dust
in your hair
to help you fly.

Otherwise,
there is a death,
too small for some to notice,
but for me a great death,
and I weep with the spirits
as we watch another soul gasp for air
in the ocean of bitterness
it calls home.

✧

✧

To M— the "willful child"
from Marj the "brat"

Hey, M——.
Let's play some tricks on Terry.
There are lots of things to do.
Here are some of my suggestions.
Maybe you can add some, too.

While we're waiting for our session
in the quiet holding room,
let's throw a wild tantrum
to dispel some of the gloom.
Before Terry checks the racket,
we'll run back to our seats,
and as he opens up his door,
make sure our hair is neat.

He'll look at us and quiz us,
"Did you two make that noise?"
We'll say, "Oh no. We didn't.
It was a couple of young boys.
They dashed into the office
throwing things and pulling hair.
They screamed and hit and shouted.
Then they ran off back downstairs."

What do you think he'll do?

Or...
we could put a pinch of cayenne in his coffee.
I'll do it when I pour myself some tea.
He'll take a drink and heavily perspire,
and then I think he'll look at you and me.

"Who us?" we'll say with casualness and guile.
"Do you think that we would do such things?"
And then we'll turn and innocently smile,
looking puzzled at the curious happenings.

What do you think he'll do?

A whoopee cushion's just a little obvious.
Thumbtacks on the chair a little mean.
A whipped cream pie more than a little messy.
Would a battery-powered squirt gun make him scream?

And if he starts to needle you
and ask you what you're feeling,
or if your lack of action he decries,
he won't believe what hit him
when we shout out, "Just shut up!"
standing there together with fire in our eyes.

What do you think he'll do?

Maybe he'll pretend
that the routine hasn't changed
and sit there looking solemn as an owl.
But we'll share a secret giggle
if he sends us to our rooms
and think up lots more mischief for tomorrow.

✧

Terry counsels, with god-like acumen,
me, a wacky, intelligent woman.
But he parties, he rocks,
wears zebra-stripped socks.
Can it be that this therapist's human?

Terry falls off his pedestal into the arms of God knows what

or

Marj and A— take another look.

✧

The marathon

First you have us stand up
and walk around the room,
looking into other people's eyes.
You do this knowing full well
that I've wandered through my life
safely staring at the sidewalk or the skies.

But my terror doesn't phase you,
I don't see you quail at all,
while I stumble through the irritating scene.
You just sit there looking patient
with a smile upon your face.
Now, don't you think that's just a little mean?

And there's all this silly touching,
rubbing backs and holding hands.
I've even seen you share a hug or two.
It really drives me crazy
watching all this gooey mush
I almost want to scream like the hyena in the zoo.

"Would you like to work on that?
Maybe jump around or bat?"
you say, knowing that I feel it in each follicle.

Then I start to scream and wail
and everyone turns pale.
Now I know that you are slightly diabolical.

We talk of aunts and fathers,
mothers, sisters, cats and brothers,
for we've all had pasts more than a little rough.
But Terry, let's be honest,
since the moment is upon us,
isn't one time through our childhood enough?

Well, I guess I have to do this,
at least once before I die.
Otherwise I'll always choke and smother.
So once the battings ended,
and the therapist I've befriended,
I'll find the guts to talk about my mother.

✧

"Are you scared?" Marj asked.
"Yes and no," Terry said. "I get scared
when I go out looking for boundaries
and they're not there."

These poems were written to Terry
over the course of several years.

✧

I need to see you needy,
to see you sad,
sitting alone in your room,
absently reading
or staring at the wall,
pulling yourself from your chair with effort,
mechanically opening the door and starting work.

In your sadness
I find safety.
In your weakness
I find strength.

I need to see you lonely,
to see you reaching out to touch
and finding no one there,
the beauty in your world diminished,
the intensity of your experience dulled
because you are alone.
I imagine you longing
for the energy I would bring into your life.

Your loneliness makes me feel loved.

Otherwise, I'm in trouble!
When I see you as a man,

see your gentleness with others,
I feel your hands on my body
touching me as a lover,
exploring my curves and creases for the first time,
knowing that my hands and heart
hold the same promise for you.

✧

✧

I did it!

We met last night
you and I.
You stood there smiling
with your hands in your pockets,
challenging me to see
you.
We pulled away the masks,
shook hands,
and said "Hello."

What do you think of that?!

✧

✧

So what's the big deal?
This is between you and me, Terry.
I knew what you were up to,
standing there smiling
with your hands in your pockets,
challenging me to trust
you.

She can talk about masks and shaking hands.
You and I met long ago,
and it's been one helluva time!
We struggle head to head,
although I make most of the racket,
screaming in corners
and threatening you with bodily harm.

Every time I look up
you're still there.
You're trying to prove something, aren't you.
Well!!!!
Don't think you can dress me in pinafores
and make me play with dolls.
I want my space,
and I'm going to take it.

If you can accept that
maybe we can call a truce.
I'll be watching you.
She and I've got some talking to do.
Then we'll see.*

*It took me two years to stop pasting my father's image on Terry. Only then could I begin to trust him.

✧

Run away with me to the palace that floats on sunbeams and soft breezes in my dreams. It's a fairy-tale palace, with crystalline towers and the music of blue bells whispering through its rooms, with magic gardens and waterfalls that shine like diamonds in the sun.

We'll eat blueberry pie and ice cream for breakfast, stuffing it in as fast as we can, make blueberry ice cream soup in our bowls, pick it up to drink, and smile at each other with blueberry ice cream moustaches and purple teeth. Then I'll go outside to play, while you stay in and do the things that grown-ups like to do.

First I'll paddle barefoot in the pond and, using lily pads for stepping stones, jump from leaf to leaf until I reach the middle. I'll sit on the petal of the largest flower and have a conversation with a frog dressed in green waistcoat and spats who is hiding in the water hoping that an insect will fly by and think that he's a plant.

"Proper children," he will say, "don't have muddy feet and dirty faces. Proper children know their 'pleases' and 'thank you's' and bow or curtsey when they say hello."

I'll laugh and catch a ride on a turquoise damselfly who will blow a silver trumpet that it keeps under one wing. Soon a thousand damselflies of blues and greens and lacy wings will join us, and we'll buzz the silly frog until he dives under the water in disgust.

Then I'll come inside, and we'll have strawberry shortcake for lunch.

After noon, we'll run hand-in-hand through fields of flowers—my little hand in yours, safe and warm—pretending that we're horses galloping through the heather, neighing and kicking up our heels. You will get a little tired and sit down in the Black-eyed Susans while I grab a milkweed parachute and float up to the clouds.

At 4 o'clock we'll have high tea with cucumber sandwiches and pastries, spreading the tablecloth out on a carpet of moss. I will do the honors, asking if you take milk, passing you your seashell cup and silver teaspoon. We'll sip our tea, talk of princesses, tin soldiers, and let the field mice clean up all the crumbs.

You will take a nap lying face up on the ground, soaking in the sun, just long enough, you say, to get refreshed. I'll wander over to the nearest waterfall and climb the rocks way up to the top, the ice-cold water splashing on my face, my toes and fingers squirming into crevices chipped away with diamond picks by rock fairies just the night before.

There I'll sit until the sun's about to set, then slide down on a rainbow and land right at your feet.

After our hot fudge sundae supper, you'll light the fire in the fireplace and sit down in your favorite chair. I will curl up in your lap, listening to stories of Pooh and Piglet or maybe silly Toad in his fancy motorcar, and fall asleep to dream of catching heffalumps or floating on the river with Otter and Mole.

You will carry me up to bed. My bedroom's the one closest to the stars. I keep the window open so they can visit when they wish. You'll fluff up my feather pillow, tuck me in and say good night, lighting a candle by my bed before you go downstairs.

And then I'll sleep, while my fairy godmother weaves me dresses from the moonlight and braids starry ribbons in my hair.

✧

✧

It was your birthday*
and they started to sing
all forty of them started to sing
and you opened yourself to receive
with a smile
you opened yourself to receive
your heart in your hand
and they started to sing
all forty of them started to sing
and they cut your heart into little pieces
letter by letter
they opened the wound deeper and deeper
hoping to see you bleed
as they sang.

If I had been there
we would have erected a shield
a shield that cut out all the songs
except our own
a shield that shattered words
words dropping like slivers of glass
that cut their tongues
and pierced their eyes
so they could see.

You left the hall
knowing that you'd wanted to cry but hadn't

*This poem was based on a story Terry told about an experience at camp as a child.

knowing that your soul was soaked with tears
that you trembled from the blows
proud they hadn't seen you cry.

And then you saw the letters in the sand.
It was premeditated murder.

If I had been there
we would have obliterated the words
kicking with our feet
grinding each of the forty singers beneath our heels.
You'd start at one end
I at the other
and we would meet in the middle
feet burning from the heat
tears streaking down our faces
strong
and raise our fists to the sky.

What a birthday party we'd have then.
I'd write letters in the sand like Charlotte in her web.
Simply wonderful Terry!
Simply terrific Terry!
Simply you! (Which is the best, I think)
and decorate my messages with curlicues and flowers
or maybe Roman rockets.

We'd look for tens of things
ten candles on a cake

ten frogs
ten snakes
ten butterflies
or climb ten feet off the ground
toes gripping the bark of trees
fingers curled 'round branches
swaying in the wind
and you'd make ten wonderful wishes
that we know would all come true.

We'd sit in the grove of pines
molding clay we'd dug up from the riverbed
pretending
we could change people
into toads
or stone
or make them melt away.

What a mess we'd be
caked with mud
pine pitch sticking to our hands and faces
scraped and bruised from climbing trees
or jumping off the sand hills.
I'd race you to the water
and we'd jump in
splashing
and kicking
and floating on our backs
'til the sun lifted us up to the sky.

Then we'd lie on the clouds
read comic books
and talk to the birds
spying on the little people running
in circles on the ground
and laugh
because it had been a glorious day after all
and we hoped it would never end.

✧

✧

The fire I built was white heat,
consuming handfuls of needles and twigs
as fast as I could feed it—
pine pitch fireworks,
fragments of exploding stones
spitting out
in unpredictable directions.

I built it to melt the numbness at my quick,
but all it did was singe the outer layer,
a good heat for Baked Alaska
but not exactly healing for the soul
although
it kept me safe.

I thought I'd try some hardwood
        apple, cherry, oak
        anything that fueled a steadier flame
and searched for windfalls,
branches pruned by heavy snows,
not rotted host of fungi
but dry and crisp,
slow to catch,
sound honest-burning logs.

We sat and talked,
you on your side,

I on mine,
warming hands and faces,
the penetrating heat
softening the sharpness of my mouth,
the terror in my eyes.
It was a birthing from the heart.

My words floated in the trembling air between us,
flower petals tossed by the wind,
caught in hot currents,
sparks glistening,
spinning round,
threatening to drift off with the smoke
like blackened ashes
disintegrating before they touched the trees.

You gathered them in
deliberately,
one by one,
and held them for awhile.
Then you gave them back,
placing
a yellow rosebud
in my hands.

✧

Terry,
I hear your voice
and the voices of others
telling me I am clean.
Thank you.

Marj

✧

I am a woman of the earth,
granite thrust up to the clouds,
a nesting place of eagles.

I scream the scream of the wildcat,
the death-cry of the rabbit.

The song of the Wood Thrush bubbles in my throat,
molten gold in the forest.

Rivers pull at my breasts,
their waters flowing down my hips and thighs
like the hands of a lover.

I am a woman of the earth.
Blackberry juices paint my lips.
Wild rose and honeysuckle grow entangled in my hair,
their heady fragrance almost cloying in its sweetness.

My womb is rich, freshly-turned soil,
humus on the forest floor,
carrying the seed of oak and violet
nestled in the warm moist softness of my body.

I am the rage of the cyclone,
trees ripped from the ground,
a swath of devastation in my wake.

My passion is the passion of the wind,
of scarlet maple in autumn,
of copper beech leaves and blue sky.

It is the passion of a freshly-dropped fawn
shivering in a bed of ferns.

I float with lake mists in early dawn;
gather nectar with the honeybees in heat of day.
My soul shimmers in the moonlight,
and I sleep in a pool of liquid silver.

I am a woman of the earth.

✧

✧

Daddy
You're an old man now,
safe enough in the eggshell of a life you've created,
held together by rituals and careful planning...
no surprises allowed.

You fix tea in the morning
and sit in bed with Penny,
peeling oranges,
your teacup clattering lightly
against the saucer as you set it down,
a vibrato of china on china.

Trying to awaken the atrophying muscles of your throat,
you preface conversation with a cough,
hesitantly
dragging words into your consciousness
as if the sound's frequency will shatter you.
Your voice trembles
I think
not with age
but with the effort.

Then you move on to your shower and breakfast.
Your job is fixing the toast,
popping it up at just the right moment,

carefully spreading it with butter
and bisecting it down the middle,
forming two perfect rectangles on your plate.
You scoop up marmalade with the tip of your knife
scraping it off on the bit of toast you plan to bite first.

The rest of the day is a series of intervals—
a hike around the lake,
sleep in the afternoon,
an evening of folk dance,
finishing with the Feldenkrais exercises
before you go to bed.

Everything seems to be done pianissimo.
Measure by measure
you live in muted tones,
following a score you've orchestrated for yourself,
a disciplined
study
of half-steps.
Only your eyes burn.

Do you remember, I wonder?
Do you remember the fire of your soul?
The times when you were scrabbling to survive,
lost in a vicious anger turned on yourself
and those of us who lived with you?
Or was the past set aside
when you changed your name from Will to Bill?

Was it packed in a suitcase weighted with cement
and dropped into the river?

How odd to think that you might work hard to forget
while I work so hard to remember.

Right now,
in this time
that changes from minute to minute,
I don't care whether you remember or forget.
I'm slowly bringing you into focus,
unifying multiple images into one.
My love
is tinged with sorrow,
my anger
softened with acceptance.

After all,
you're just a man
who's trying to live,
a shadow
plotting out your movements in advance,
placing your elbows
carefully
on the table
so as not
to rattle
the glasses.

✧

✧

How could such a small truth
shatter the twisted construct of my world?
One soft blow on the fragile shell,
and its fragments fell at my feet,
momentarily walling me in
before they dropped away.

Etchings of a life
burned in the surface with the acid of betrayal
lay in pieces,
remnants of a time
when I crawled in the shells of other people
because my truth was too hard to bear.

But,
of course,
I have always borne my truth,
buried inside
in the voice of the child,
who was faced with the torment of histories
that never were told,
who managed to keep afloat in suffering's passion
before she even learned to read.

The wisdom of the woman
was there in the child all along.

She was the teacher in this
with her love
and sorrow
and belief in fairy godmothers.

That is why I want to see things simply,
why my words
when they flow freely
are childlike.
Because the essence of it all was there with her,
and she was only six.

As I've washed away
the grit of my life,
I've found
a simple pearl of a child
who sees far beyond the pain
and knows how to love.

✧

Dear Reader,

I haven't written gently. Rage isn't sweet and unoffending. This is not the oily secret stuff I fell victim to as a child. This is the sword-swinging, knife-wielding, fist-held-high power of a woman. I came alive with the fire of my soul. My passions were born with screams and blows, and my little girl could sing again.

With time, swift waters carve deep canyons in the earth. We stand at the edge and look into the depths, admiring sculpted stone bridges and rounded formations, trying to glimpse the undercurrents and boulders beneath the river's surface. Blinded by reflections of sun-off-water, we forget the tearing power of birth.

But I will not forget. I am the granite and the cyclone of my poems. I am the violets and the roses of my poems. I am the whittler, the warrior. And I will not be rounded off and polished.

For 46 years I was lost in fantasies, confused as to why I had such difficulty being real. Now I look down periodically and see that my feet are planted on Mother Earth, or at least on a tree limb, and that the rest of me is connected to those feet. Everything seems smaller and more manageable. Knowing my own boundaries as a separate person, I don't spend days scraping myself off the ceiling or dragging myself out of the quicksand.

The poems in this book help me find my truth. I hold them in cupped hands as I would a newborn kitten or a budding peony. At times I bury my nose in their fragrance, and my blood runs hot. At times I am afraid because I don't quite know what they are, and then I look deeply to the silent waiting child of my youth and know that they are of her.

Achieving separation from my writing has been difficult, but I finally believe that feelings don't have to succeed in the marketplace in order to be validated. What a change! At the watershed age of fifty, I'm coming into my own. I write when and what I want to write. I dance when and how I want to dance. I live the way I choose.

Do I forgive my father?

No.

Do I accept the past?

Yes.

With that acceptance comes some peace of spirit.

Writing this book had brought me personal power and fulfillment. I hope reading it brings you closer to yourself, into your silence and through your sorrow and anger to a space in which you can hold your own child's hand and dance with the wind.

Marj

Letters

I have decided to include these letters as an appendix to the book. I am still somewhat confused as to why I have chosen to do so. They certainly are not a fairy-tale ending to my story.

When I reread them, I berate myself. What is this "Dear" business? Why in God's name do I mention my summer vacation? Why do I tell him I would be "petrified" to talk with him?

In my mind I am not measuring up to my image of the model survivor talking with the abuser. I should have done it differently.

Well, I didn't. When I wrote the letters, that is the place I was in. That's what this healing business is all about, isn't it? Knowing where we are and acting from that place as honestly as we can? If I were writing them now, there are parts I would change. There are also many parts I would leave the same.

My reaction to my father's response has been an affirmation of my truth. That might not make sense to you, once you read his letters. It does to me. I listened to what he had to say. Then I listened to myself. And I found myself at peace.

I have had to edit some of my letters because of space constraints, deleting sentences that were repetitive or unnecessary. I do not think that the deletions have in anyway changed the intent or the voice of the letters.

✧ ✧ ✧

January ?, 1991

Dear Bill, (I am struggling with what to call you. Daddy seems so little girlish, Dad sound awkward. Thought I would try to call you what you decided you wanted people to call you.)

For the last three years I have been in therapy in an attempt to dispel some of the anxiety, confusion and undirected anger I was experiencing. I was not functioning as a healthy adult and was feeling quite unhappy and unconnected much of the time.

It has been an extremely productive three years for me. I feel like I've finally grown up. In the course of my work, I began to have flashes into the past. As you might or might not know, I remembered very little of my childhood until I was twelve or thirteen when you left home for the last time. I remember that very clearly—you coming to my room to give me a card explaining why you and Mummy were getting divorced.

My flashes of remembrances have been brief and intense, connected to rather overwhelming feelings of fear, self-disgust, love and rage. You are at the center of most of them. Until recently I had no idea how much I loved you and how much I feared and hated you. Some people might not be able to understand how all these feelings can co-exist, but I think you can, given your own childhood experiences and your struggle to achieve a life that was peaceful, safe and satisfying.

Well, I might as well just say it bluntly: I have remembered how much I loved you as a child. I have remembered that there was some sort of sexual contact between you and me. I feel that you touched me sexually and had me touch you.

I have hesitated until now to say anything about this to you because I needed to feel some sense of resolution in myself, needed to feel strong. I am at that point now, although I still have moments of doubt and fear about talking with you. At times I feel that I need to protect you somehow, that if I upset you something terrible will happen. That might be so, but I can no longer continue on pretending. I can no longer take responsibility for how you might react or feel or what you might do. I'm tired of running away and hiding. I have no desire to falsely accuse you. But I have to believe what my mind and body tell me.

If you choose to discuss this with me, I would certainly like that. If not, that is fine, also. Should you have difficulty talking with me about this, I would like to try to create a space where we can talk about talking about it. All I can say is that there was a past relationship and is a present relationship. I would hope that recognition of the first will not necessitate destruction of the second. I no longer believe it is necessary to block out unhappy times in order to live and create.

You will find enclosed a few poems I have written over the last three years. They will tell you better than any other way what my innermost feelings and torments have been. I hope if you start reading them you will read them all. They represent my growth toward mental health and resolution of my feelings toward you. If you are interested in reading more, let me know and I will send them to you.

Marj

✧ ✧ ✧

(This first letter from my father was enclosed in a card decorated with doves of peace. On it was inscribed the following excerpt from a poem by John Greenleaf Whittier, 1848:

Then shall all shackles fall; the stormy clangor
Of wild war music o'er the earth shall cease;
Love shall tread out the baleful fire of anger,
And in its ashes plant the tree of peace.)

Feb. 20, 1991

Dear Marj,

To send me a poem sneering at, and making fun of, my life-style is a cruel, brutal, destructive thing to do. (At least, that's how it struck me. Perhaps you don't realize how devastating it is to have one's life-style ridiculed.) Since the subject is irrelevant, the only possible object that I can see is to hurt me. If you are full of rage and hate, that is no doubt what you want to do. But it seems a funny way to open a discussion designed to improve communication & feeling between us. We like our life-style, which is designed for enjoying life in spite of the limitations of old age.

As for the sexual abuse accusations, I have no recollection of any such incidents. Either they are fantasies, or I have a bad case of amnesia, which I think is very unlikely. I can think of several possible uses for these fantasies, so if you want to or need to believe in them, go ahead; I believe they didn't happen.

I wouldn't want to talk to you about all this, & rake it all up again, because: (1) it would require a family therapist, which isn't practical; (2) with your letter as an example, I wouldn't want to speak freely with you, and I would not expect a satisfactory outcome; (3) it's dangerous—the doctor threatens me with a stroke or another heart attack if I let my blood pressure get up to the levels your letter provokes; (4) a therapist could help you better than I can.*

Your poems are very powerful, & bring back the experiences of those times very vividly & persistently.

Bill

**How about your blood pressure too?*

✧ ✧ ✧

3/10/91

Dear Bill,

I received your letter today. You were direct, straightforward, and you have made it clear that you do not wish to discuss this issue further. I respect that decision.

I would like to comment on your reaction to the poem in which I describe your life-style. I hope you do not consider this a violation of your wish for no further discussion about the past. As I think about what I wrote, I can see why you might have felt it as an attack.

The irony is that I included the poem to somehow soften the rest of the material. It was written from a place of sadness, love, pride and some sort of understanding. I am sad that you felt I was just ridiculing your life and that you felt my only purpose for writing it was to hurt you.

You say that the subject of the piece was irrelevant. It wasn't to me. One of your many gifts to me has been the graceful manner with which you have aged. You and Penny and Mom have all played a role in my lack of fear about aging. I envision my old age as vital, exciting. Hikes, music, exercises, dancing are pleasures that I enjoy in my own life now and plan to for many years to come. When I wrote the poem, I originally had included a long list of your activities and interests. I was saying, look at this. Look at the things he does! And he is in his eighties! Artistically it didn't work, and so I cut here and there in order to capture just the essence.

It is hard to pick just one part of my life that I see as being strongly influenced by you and your way of thinking. Music, of course, is very dominant. The pleasure you obviously gain from exploring many forms from classical to folk to whatever takes your fancy has taught me so much. I still remember the day we came to visit you and you had us all sit in a circle on the floor and sing Pete Seeger's "Garbage (garbage, garbage, garbage) Song."

Moments like that gave me permission to play (in all senses of the word). Tomorrow night I am throwing a rhythm and blues party to celebrate my 50th birthday. I've written a song and have been desperately attempting to learn to do a piano blues as backup. My friend Geoff, who plays a great guitar, is my mentor and guitar back-up in this effort. And where did I get the unspoken OK to attempt such an effort? From you.

My willingness to experiment with alternative methods of healing and relaxation stems directly from you. In your own struggle to maintain a healthy relaxed life, with your Feldenkrais exercises and the Alexander technique, you have moved far beyond conventional boundaries in your thinking. The fact that you do Feldenkrais exercises in the evening is not a point of ridicule. I am envious. Just as I am envious of your tradition of having tea in bed in the morning. I hope the day will come when my family and I will find the balance and little pleasures you have built into your life.

You have a special ability to play—with ideas, with music, with nature, with consciousness. The effects of such a mind set are sometimes painful and sometimes beautiful, sometimes frightening and sometimes exciting. It leads to a life of passion. For the part you have played in modeling that perspective on life for me, I thank you.

Marj

✧ ✧ ✧

March 23, 1991

Dear Marj,

When I received your second letter, I was about to write to say that it would be a pity if we ended up not on speaking terms. In your first letter you suggested that we might at least talk about talking about what happened. I can see that you have been very distressed about your childhood, but it seems to me that it's a matter between you & your therapist, that for you & me to talk about it would not only be painful but would only make matters worse.

Talking about therapists, it seems that you are wanting to throw a new light on your personal history—to "reframe" it, in the words of the NLP people. They claim to have developed very quick & relatively painless methods of doing this, based on studying how the most effective therapists, such as Virginia Satir, achieve their results.

Perhaps I'll be able to reframe your life-style poem as appreciation rather than ridicule.

Bill

✧ ✧ ✧

August 9, 1991

Dear Bill,

Jean told me awhile ago that she told you I was planning to publish my work. I know I agreed not to discuss this further with you, but I can't really leave it up in the air as it is now. Ever since your letter indicating you found it too upsetting to rake up the past, I've been debating how to handle this particular issue.

I have a manuscript that is almost completed. It consists of a series of poems and a couple essay-type prose pieces that I have written over the past three years. Included are the poems I sent you. The decision re publication has been very hard to make. The issues are obvious. On the other hand, I am proud of my work. People have told me it helps them deal with their own childhood sorrows, whatever they might be. They say there is a universality about the poems that touches them.

It has taken me a year to decide what name to use. I have felt uncertain about publishing under my name, yet part of me has felt angry that I would consider not using my name. I have decided to publish under the name of Marj. This would ease the pressure for everyone in the family, and I certainly do not have the desire to introduce further pain into an already painful situation.

I have discussed all of this at length with Mom, Jean and Mary.

They have had feelings about it—about the fact that I say you stepped beyond appropriate bounds sexually with me when I was a child and about the fact that I am going to publish a book.

Now I have a question that you might consider to be totally off the wall, but I want to ask it. I have debated about whether to, or how to, include your point of view as you expressed in your first letter to me. I've been back and forth. After all, this book is a collection of poems that express my feelings. Does any more belong? I don't know. I don't want to turn it into "did you or didn't you."

On the other hand, the book is about growth and communication. You had several options when you received my first letter. You chose to think it through and respond as honestly as possible. I appreciate that you did that. Could I have permission to use your letters, or at least parts of your letters, in a "Letters" section at the end of the book? Your identity would be protected. I will not use anything you wrote if you don't want me to. You would also have control over what parts I would include.

Thank you for your second letter. I know you are trying to communicate with me. Here I go, dropping another bombshell. I don't know whether we will be able to struggle past this one. I'm willing to try, but I don't quite know how it will work.

I hope your summer has gone well. We are headed up to Main for 9 days for some camping, some B & B..

Marj

✧ ✧ ✧

Aug. 18, 1991

Dear Marj,

Thank you for offering to include my responses in your book.

Naturally, I would prefer you not to publish the book at all. In fact, it seems incredible that you would want to. If you do, perhaps it would be better to present it as fictional, or partly fictional, in view of my denial that these episodes ever took place. In this case, it would be inappropriate to include the letters,

If you do publish it as autobiographical, as implied in the "Dear Reader" part, the letters (your first and my replies) should be included in full. Publishing parts of them would undoubtedly distort their meaning.

Bill

✧ ✧ ✧

Aug. 19, 1991

Dear Marj,

It seems to me that the addition of a foreword would be a much more satisfactory solution than including the letters. It can tell the readers all they need to know in a few words.

Bill

FOREWORD

Marj believes that the sexual molestation episodes described in this book really happened. I, her father, know that they did not. I have heard that such fantasies are not uncommon. They presumably satisfy some psychological needs.

On the other hand, the feelings of love, hate and rage expressed so powerfully in these poems are real enough.

Her father

✧ ✧ ✧

8-23-91

Dear Bill,

Thanks for giving me, initially, permission to use your two letters. Guess my asking wasn't as off-the-wall as I thought.

I wanted to include your letters so that people could know your side and also see that talking about this stuff isn't easy. You were so honest in them. We've never talked like this to each other before. (Actually, I am finding it easier doing it in letters rather than face to face. I think I could sit across table and talk with you about how I am feeling, but I would be petrified. It took me more than a year to write you the first letter.) I do think that our letters could help women and men explore their own issues.

I was disappointed when you wrote that you didn't think the letters were satisfactory after all. The foreword you sent is certainly direct. I can understand why you want such a clear-cut statement; however, it seems so cold, so devoid of personality.

How would you feel about me using all three? That is, the first and second letters you wrote as well as the statement?

Marj

✧ ✧ ✧

Sept. 3, 1991

Dear Marj,

It's not that the letters were "unsatisfactory"—it's just that they seemed to be a private matter between us, so I suggested the "foreword" as a substitute. There doesn't seem to be much point in the foreword if you publish the other letters as well,

However, it's for you to decide. Publish either the letters, or the foreword, or both.

Bill

✧ ✧ ✧

Dear Reader,

Do you see what I mean? The letters are not a fairy-tale ending. But I'm still here.

I didn't write to my father until I felt strong enough to handle his response. In fact, I didn't write until I had set aside all hope for a particular answer. You know what I'm talking about. Where he would write back: "Oh yes, Marj, it happened. I'm so sorry, and I'll do whatever I can to help us work through the pain!"

I tried to create a space in which he and I could talk. He chose not to step into that clearing. We haven't shut down the possibility of future communication, but my thought right now is: "What do we have to talk about? On what ground can we meet?"

His letters stirred me up; they didn't blow me away. And I continue to mourn the loss of the father I never really had.

Would I have written to him if I had not been planning to publish this book?

I don't know. Confrontation was not a goal of mine. Some people say it is important for healing; some disagree. I'm learning that there is not one right path to follow.

Which brings me to you. We meet in a place that is beyond words, a place of unity and support, not isolation. Each time we touch in spirit, we grow stronger. Thank you for joining me there.

Marj